THE
CUMBRIA
QUIZ BOOK

First Edition

Visit www.facebook.com/petemossbooks

ABOUT THE AUTHOR

Pete Moss has been at radio station CFM in Carlisle since 1997, joining the local commercial broadcaster straight out of school at the age of 17. As well as being a presenter, his further role of Content Director has seen him create many contests and quizzes for all shows on the station.

He is the only current CFM presenter to have grown up in Cumbria. Pete was born in Penrith and lived his first few years in a cottage owned by Beatrix Potter's brother-in-law in Appleby before moving to Carlisle at the age of 3.

He attended Stanwix and Belah Primary Schools gaining secondary education at Trinity School. Throughout childhood Pete developed a love for music and radio creating his own pretend radio station and writing his own songs.

During his time on CFM he has produced and presented many shows including the locally focussed Saturday programme *The Cumberland Sausage Show* and the weekday daytime show he still presents today.

Pete has hosted many of the county's major events including Carlisle's Bitts Park Fire Show for 3 years, big name concerts at the Whitehaven Festival and numerous Christmas lights switch ons in Cumbria. He has even been a judge at the World Gurning Championships in Egremont!

INTRODUCTION

Since the first lockdown during the coronavirus pandemic more people have got into quizzing. Virtual quizzes gave purpose to family, friends and work colleagues getting together via group video chats online. The preparation of questions is something I was already very used to thanks to writing many for various contests on CFM over the years, but it has only ever been 10 questions here, 10 questions there – never quite as many as feature in this quiz book!

During the initial lockdown I put together a week of quizzing for CFM that was entirely about Cumbria, as it would be something that tapped into the increased quizzing being enjoyed at home, but was also a unique and very relevant subject for our listeners who love being tested on their local knowledge. CFM achieved its highest online weekly listening figures while this Cumbrian quiz was on air.

This inspired me to investigate whether I could expand on the questions I had written to put together a whole book of Cumbria quizzes. Under normal circumstances I would never have had the time to spend on researching and writing so many questions, but being confined to the house for much of 2020 has provided the opportunity to create a huge collection of questions on Cumbria to make a book.

It always seems that books on Cumbria focus on the fells, the lakes and its Roman history, but I wanted this quiz book to be more than just that. Indeed, all of that IS covered in the questions featured, but there is also plenty about Cumbria now and its recent history. Whether it is reminiscing about shops that used to be in The Lanes or testing our knowledge of some of the people who are flying the flag for Cumbria through their achievements in sport, TV, film, literature and music, this book should have something for everyone who knows a thing or two about Cumbria, no matter what they're interested in.

And it's not just straight questions, there are quizzes featuring pictures to identify, cryptic puzzles to solve and anagrams to decipher. To make the book even more enjoyable and easy to use you don't have to go hunting around for the answers – you'll find them printed on the edge of the page overleaf.

I hope you have fun testing your knowledge of all things Cumbria, or challenging your friends, family and work colleagues with the questions in this book. It's been a lot of fun researching and writing it and I have learned a lot along the way, I dare say there will be a fair few things about Cumbria YOU will also discover reading it.

LANDMARKS

Some of the county's most recognisable places

1	Which Carlisle landmark was the tallest of its kind in Europe when built in 1836?
2	What is the name of the mechanical clock in Workington town centre?
3	In 2019 the Cumbria Pride concert took place at which Cumbrian landmark for the first time?
4	Which town is overlooked by a landmark known as 'The Candlestick'?
5	What is the name of the stone circle located near Keswick?
6	Which Ambleside house was the home of William Wordsworth until his death in 1850?
7	What is the name of the large stone in Borrowdale where visitors often shake hands beneath?
8	A 1981 an archaeological dig in the grounds of which landmark uncovered a well-preserved body who became known as 'St Bees Man'?
9	Which town's small lighthouse has been depicted in many paintings by L.S. Lowry?
10	Which Ulverston monument honours explorer Sir John Barrow?

In this section at the edge of the page you will find the answers to the quiz from a page-turn back. So, you will see the answers to quiz 1 in the grey section beside quiz 3

TRAVEL

Questions about transport links past and present

1	What mode of transport disappeared from Carlisle for good in 1931?
2	What is the full name of Penrith's train station?
3	Which train operator manages Carlisle Railway Station?
4	What is the full name of Carlisle Airport?
5	In which street would you find Carlisle's bus station?
6	How was Oxenholme's train station renamed in 1988?
7	What mode of transport disappeared from Silloth in 1964?
8	What was the name of the bus company who operated in Cumbria before being taken over by Stagecoach in 1989?
9	Safety concerns over which derelict building caused major Carlisle route Victoria Viaduct to be closed for long periods between 2018-2020?
10	When Carlisle Lake District Airport opened a new terminal for passenger flights in July 2019, to which three cities could you fly?

In this section at the edge of the page you will find the answers to the quiz from a page-turn back. So, you will see the answers to quiz 2 in the grey section beside quiz 4

ANSWERS QUIZ 1

1	Dixon's Chimney
2	Look Out
3	Carlisle Castle
4	Whitehaven
5	Castlerigg Stone Circle
6	Rydal Mount
7	Bowder Stone
8	St Bees Priory
9	Maryport
10	Hoad Monument

FAMOUS CUMBRIANS (1)

The well-known folk from the county

1	Of which boy band was Carlisle-born singer Lee Brennan a member?
2	Which Cumbrian has been played by Errol Flynn, Clark Gable, Marlon Brando and Mel Gibson in movies?
3	Which comedy actor was born in Ulverston as Arthur Stanley Jefferson?
4	Which Fleetwood Mac singer was born in the village of Bouth?
5	What was the name of the Carlisle choir boy who reached the final of *Britain's Got Talent* in 2008?
6	Which Workington-born England international Rugby Union player retired from the sport in 2015?
7	Penrith-born actress Angela Lonsdale played Curly Watts' wife Emma in which TV soap?
8	Which Cumbrian-born physicist introduced the atomic theory into chemistry?
9	Which Cumbrian was the presenter of ITV's *The South Bank Show*?
10	Which poet was born in Cockermouth in 1770?

#	Question		Answer
1	Which Carlisle actress played Jo Sugden in *Emmerdale*?	1	Tram
2	Which Carlisle-born singer represented the UK in the 2000 Eurovision Song Contest?	2	Penrith North Lakes
3	Which artist from Aspatria sold out her first London exhibition and was good friends with L.S. Lowry?	3	Avanti West Coast
4	Which lady from Kirkby Thore became a *Blue Peter* presenter in 2008?	4	Carlisle Lake District Airport
5	Carlisle-born David King represented Great Britain at the 2010 and 2014 Winter Olympics in which sport?	5	Lonsdale Street
6	Carlisle's Matt Pagan won *Britain's Got Talent* in 2014 as part of which vocal group?	6	Oxenholme Lake District
7	In what sport did Ulverston-born Norman Gifford represent England?	7	Train
8	Which Carlisle-born actor played Ernie Wise in the 2011 BBC TV film *Eric & Ernie*?	8	Ribble
9	Maryport-born Bunty James was a presenter on which children's television show in the 1960s and 1970s?	9	The Central Plaza Hotel
10	Kendal-born singer Steve Hogarth replaced Fish as lead vocalist of which band in 1989?	10	Belfast, Dublin and London

ATTRACTIONS (1)
The places tourists love to visit

QUIZ
5

1	911
2	Fletcher Christian
3	Stan Laurel
4	Christine McVie
5	Andrew Johnston
6	Mark Cueto
7	*Coronation Street*
8	John Dalton
9	Melvyn Bragg
10	William Wordsworth

1	In 1998, Jefferson's Wine Merchants closed in Whitehaven. Which tourist attraction now stands in its former Lowther Street premises?
2	What name is given to the big stone displayed in Carlisle's Millennium Gallery?
3	In which Cumbrian town would you find the tourist attraction 'The Puzzling Place'?
4	What is the name of the forest where Center Parcs is located in Cumbria?
5	What is the proper name of Maryport's aquarium?
6	In which Keswick forest would you find a Go Ape adventure centre?
7	Which Cumbrian museum has the skeletal structure of a whale called Driggsby on display?
8	Which hall at Kendal claims to have the world's largest and oldest topiary gardens in its grounds?
9	Which body of water is the Lake District's ONLY true lake?
10	In which Cumbrian town would you find Wordsworth House?

#	Question		Answer
1	What attraction in Keswick is based around optical illusions?	1	Roxanne Pallett
2	What is the name of William Wordsworth's cottage on the edge of Grasmere?	2	Nicki French
3	At which Workington entertainment centre could you play ten-pin bowling?	3	Sheila Fell
4	West Coast Indoor Karting can be found in which town?	4	Helen Skelton
5	Which attraction sees water falling from Aira Beck down a 65-foot drop?	5	Figure skating
6	Which heritage railway is known locally as La'al Ratty?	6	Collabro
7	Which indoor climbing centre is based in Kendal?	7	Cricket
8	Which zoo on the outskirts of Dalton-in-Furness was formerly known as South Lakes Wild Animal Park?	8	Bryan Dick
9	Which Penrith attraction is often referred to as 'the village in the hill'?	9	How
10	Which farm park just outside Carlisle boasts Cumbria's largest indoor play area	10	Marillion

ANSWERS QUIZ 5

			ANAGRAMS (1) Rearrange the letters to get a Cumbrian place name
1	The Rum Story	1	Have The Win
2	Cursing Stone	2	Check Our Tom
3	Keswick	3	Nut Lovers
4	Whinfell Forest	4	More Cola Rot
5	Lake District Coast Aquarium	5	My Parrot
6	Whinlatter	6	Her Pint
7	Tullie House	7	No Wet Baby
8	Levens Hall	8	Disable Me
9	Lake Bassenthwaite (the others are waters, meres or tarns)	9	Ban Mr Pot
10	Cockermouth	10	Wood Barrel

ANAGRAMS (2)

Rearrange the letters to get a
Cumbrian place name

ANSWERS
QUIZ 6

1	Weirder Men
2	Mr Get One
3	Mr Nutcase
4	Bald Kinky Loser
5	Navel Grass
6	Case Ales
7	Ill Shot
8	My Two Bleepers
9	True Walls
10	Dragons Avengers

1	The Puzzling Place
2	Dove Cottage
3	Eclipse Leisure Centre
4	Maryport
5	Aira Force
6	Ravenglass and Eskdale Railway
7	Kendal Wall, Lakeland Climbing Centre
8	South Lakes Safari Zoo
9	The Rheged Centre
10	Walby Farm Park

STATUES

Questions on sculptures honouring events or people

1	Whitehaven	1	A statue of which monarch is situated in Bitts Park, Carlisle?
2	Cockermouth	2	Which comedy duo's statues stand on Victoria Road in Ulverston?
3	Ulverston	3	Renee Zellweger visited Cumbria in 2006 to unveil a statue of which author?
4	Cleator Moor	4	Which Lord is honoured with a statue on Main Street, Cockermouth?
5	Maryport	5	A statue of which film monster stood for a few years at Skirsgill Auction Mart in Penrith from 2005?
6	Penrith	6	What is the name of the violinist who sits outside Debenhams in the Lanes, Carlisle?
7	Abbeytown	7	A statue celebrating which traditional local sport stood near Workington's Curwen Hall until it was vandalised in 2012?
8	Ambleside	8	The Kendal War Memorial Statue in Market Square depicts a soldier serving in which war?
9	Brampton	9	Which 19th century Carlisle mayor is immortalised in a statue that stands outside Marks & Spencer on English Street in the city?
10	Borrowdale	10	A statue of which American naval officer spiking canons is situated on Whitehaven harbour?

#	Question		Answer
1	Cumbria contains England's longest body of water, what is it?	1	Windermere
2	The highest mountain in England is situated in Cumbria, what is it?	2	Egremont
3	Which Cumbrian town was the first in the UK to have analog TV switched off and go fully digital?	3	Muncaster
4	Which Cumbrian was Google's 2nd most-searched for celebrity in 2018?	4	Kirkby Lonsdale
5	In which Carlisle street is it believed the first mainland post box in the UK was erected in 1853?	5	Ravenglass
6	Which Cumbrian town is reportedly the first place in the UK where police used riot gear?	6	Seascale
7	Which hill pass in Cumbria is England's joint-steepest road?	7	Silloth
8	What English record can Wast Water at Wasdale claim to hold?	8	Temple Sowerby
9	Where in Cumbria is the joint-highest market town in England with Buxton in Derbyshire?	9	Ullswater
10	Which town's canal claims to be the straightest in the UK?	10	Grange-over-Sands

ANSWERS QUIZ 9	

ANSWERS QUIZ 9

POSTMAN PAT
How much do you know about the fictional Cumbrian postman?

QUIZ 11

	ANSWERS			QUESTIONS
1	Queen Victoria		1	What is Pat's surname?
2	Laurel & Hardy		2	Which valley near Kendal was the inspiration for Greendale?
3	Beatrix Potter		3	At which Kendal primary school was *Postman Pat* creator Jon Cunliffe teaching when he wrote the first stories?
4	Lord Mayo (Richard Southwell Bourke)		4	What was the name of Pat's black and white cat?
5	King Kong		5	Who ran the Greendale post office?
6	Jimmy Dyer		6	What is the name of the nearby fictional town where Pat collects the parcels to deliver in the *Special Delivery Service* spin-off series?
7	Uppies & Downies		7	What is the name of Pat's son?
8	World War I		8	Which famous singer provided Pat's singing voice in the 2014 film *Postman Pat: The Movie*?
9	James Steel		9	Who is Greendale's resident handyman and inventor?
10	John Paul Jones		10	Who provided the voice of all the characters in the very first series of *Postman Pat*?

SHOPPING

Questions about supermarkets,
stores and shopping centres

1	In which Cumbrian shopping centre would you find the Plaza Cinema?
2	Which Ambleside garden centre bears the name of the family of gardeners who started the business?
3	Which is the only supermarket chain to have 3 stores in Carlisle?
4	Which clothing store now occupies the shop unit where BHS used to be in Carlisle city centre?
5	Which Carlisle department store do many local people still refer to as 'Binns'?
6	Which department store in Carlisle opened its doors in 1910 and closed them for a final time in 2006?
7	Workington town centre's main shopping square shares its name with which American state?
8	Which is the only one of the UK's top 10 supermarkets not to have a store in Cumbria?
9	In which Cumbrian town would you be if you were shopping in Devonshire Arcade?
10	In which Kendal shopping centre can you find Poundland, The Body Shop and Grape Tree?

1	Windermere
2	Scafell Pike
3	Whitehaven
4	Roxanne Pallet
5	Botchergate
6	Keswick
7	Hardknott Pass
8	Deepest lake
9	Alston
10	Ulverston

FOOD AND DRINK

From famous Cumbrian foods to places to eat and drink

QUIZ 13

1	Clifton
2	Longsleddale
3	Castle Park School
4	Jess
5	Mrs Goggins
6	Pencaster
7	Julian
8	Ronan Keating
9	Ted Glen
10	Ken Barrie

1	For which baked food stuff is the village of Grasmere famous?
2	What brand of table water biscuits are made in Carlisle?
3	Which fish 'n' chip shop has stood in Whitehaven's marketplace since 1908?
4	Which well-known fruit juice drink was created in the Cumbrian village of Milnthorpe?
5	Which dessert would you associate with The Sharrow Bay Country House hotel near Pooley Bridge?
6	Which Cumbrian food was granted 'protected geographical indication' status in 2011, meaning that only when it is prepared in Cumbria can it be named 'traditional'?
7	Well known for its patties, which long-established Denton Holme fish 'n' chip shop closed in 2018 after its owner suffered an injury making it too difficult to continue?
8	Which famous Cumbrian confection is made by companies Romney's and Quiggin's?
9	In Carlisle, what do John Watt and Bruce & Luke's specialise in?
10	Casa A Roma in Whitehaven, Tarantella in Cockermouth and Michelangelos in Carlisle all specialise in the cuisine of what country?

#	Question	#	Answer
1	Which Labour Party leader officially opened The Sands Centre?	1	Dunmail Park
2	In what year did The Sands Centre open?	2	Hayes Garden World
3	Which singer made a surprise appearance at a Paul Weller Sands Centre concert in the 90s?	3	Aldi
4	What is the name of The Sands Centre's cafe?	4	Primark
5	Which girl group performed at the Sands Centre as part of their 'Headlines Tour' in February 2011	5	House Of Fraser
6	While The Sands Centre was redeveloped, fitness activities were relocated to which former school building in 2020?	6	Bulloughs
7	In what month of the year do The Sands Centre usually host an annual team quiz?	7	Washington
8	Which Stone Roses singer played a solo gig at The Sands Centre in November 2007?	8	Waitrose
9	Which kids TV show hosted by Stu Francis was filmed at The Sands Centre in the late 1980s?	9	Penrith
10	What important role does The Sands Centre play during elections?	10	Westmorland Shopping Centre

ANSWERS
QUIZ 13

1	Gingerbread
2	Carr's
3	Arrighis
4	Um Bongo
5	Sticky Toffee Pudding
6	Cumberland Sausage
7	Pieri's
8	Kendal Mint Cake
9	Coffee
10	Italy

NAMES OF WHAT?
What kind of places are these?

1	What are Footsteps in Workington, Kiddlywinks in Penrith and Little Owls in Carlisle?
2	Gaiety, Alhambra and Plaza are all names of what in Cumbria?
3	St Begh's, St Mary's and St Benedict's are all names of what in Whitehaven?
4	The Ring o' Bells, The New Union and Romneys are all names of what in Kendal?
5	What are Chapel, Sonatas and The Strand in Carlisle?
6	Seabreeze, Ocean and The Old Smithy in Barrow-in-Furness are all names of what kind of shop?
7	What are St Michael's, St John's and Saint Gregory's in Workington?
8	Sykeside at Hartsop, Fisherground at Eskdale and Kestrel Lodge at Keswick are all what?
9	What are St Columba's, Brisbane Park and Sacred Heart in Barrow-in-Furness?
10	What kind of businesses are Ruby's in Kendal, Happy Haven in Whitehaven and Sunrise in Carlisle?

ANSWERS
QUIZ 14

1	Which Carlisle-born footballer managed England's under 20s World Cup winning team in 2017?
2	In 2020, which Cumbrian football club made their return to the English Football League after 48 years?
3	Which Cumbrian football club used to play their home games at The World Group Stadium?
4	In which decade did Workington AFC last play in the football league?
5	Which footballer from Barrow-in-Furness was also a team captain on the TV show *A Question Of Sport*?
6	In the 90s, Carlisle United's red, white and green-striped away strip was given what nickname?
7	Who did Carlisle-born footballer Kevin Beattie play for when he was awarded Professional Footballers' Association Young Player of the Year at the end of the 1972–73 season?
8	Which Whitehaven-born goalkeeper made his Premier League debut for Leeds United in 2004?
9	Which Cumbrian turned down a move to Manchester United from Carlisle United before signing for Crystal Palace in 1998?
10	Who were Carlisle United playing when goalkeeper Jimmy Glass scored his last-minute goal that saved them from going out of the football league in 1999?

#	Answer
1	Neil Kinnock
2	1985
3	Noel Gallagher
4	No. 10
5	The Saturdays
6	Newman School
7	January
8	Ian Brown
9	*Crush A Grape*
10	It becomes a count venue

GOVERNANCE

MPs, councils and general authority

QUIZ 17

1	Nurseries
2	Cinemas
3	Schools
4	Pubs
5	Hairdressers
6	Fish 'n' chip shop
7	Churches
8	Campsites
9	Primary schools
10	Chinese takeaways

1	What is the name of the Cumbrian MP who became leader of the Liberal Democrats in 2015?
2	Cumbria is represented by how many different Members of Parliament?
3	Which district council is the local authority for Penrith?
4	Who was Appleby's MP when he became Prime Minister in 1783?
5	A 'man' of which Cumbrian town was used as a political term during the 2019 election to describe the typical swing voter who could determine the result?
6	Which Prime Minister claimed in a 2005 newspaper column he wrote that he was almost beaten-up in a pub on Botchergate?
7	Who became the first female MP to represent a Cumbrian constituency in 2015?
8	In which town are the offices of South Lakeland District Council?
9	Which constituency of Cumbria is the only one this century to be represented by an independent MP?
10	What was the name of Carlisle's MP from 1987-2010?

#	Question	#	Answer
1	The name of which Cumbrian village is said to be made up of three words meaning 'hill', so literally translates as 'hill hill hill'?	1	Paul Simpson
2	Which part of the body goes after Raughton, Hawks and Nent to make place names in Cumbria?	2	Barrow AFC
3	Which town is named after the wife of Humphrey Senhouse, who founded the port there?	3	Penrith
4	Which Carlisle river's name means 'cold river'?	4	1970s (1977)
5	How many villages and hamlets are there in Cumbria with 'Newbiggin' in their name?	5	Emlyn Hughes
6	The meaning of which body of water's name is 'lake by dairy pastures'?	6	Deckchair
7	The name of which town is believed to mean 'farm where cheese is made' in Old English?	7	Ipswich Town
8	There are two Cumbrian town names beginning with S, one is Silloth, what is the other?	8	Scott Carson
9	The name of which area of Cumbria means 'land of the people living west of the moors'?	9	Matt Jansen
10	Why is the town of Cockermouth so called?	10	Plymouth Argyle

PUBS

All about drinking establishments in Cumbria

#	Answer
1	Tim Farron
2	6
3	Eden
4	William Pitt the Younger
5	Workington
6	Boris Johnson
7	Sue Hayman
8	Kendal
9	Barrow and Furness (John Woodcock)
10	Eric Martlew

1	The Bransty Arch in Whitehaven and Woodrow Wilson in Carlisle are part of which pub chain?
2	The Griffin pub in Carlisle was formerly a branch of which bank?
3	In which town would you find the pubs The Candlestick and Whittington Cat?
4	Which architect designed a number of Carlisle pubs including one that bears his name in Etterby?
5	The Workington pub Oily's was previously known by what longer name?
6	Both Carlisle and Brampton have pubs called The Howard... what?
7	In which Cumbrian town would you find the Ring o' Bells pub?
8	Carlisle, Penrith and Barrow-in-Furness all have inns named after which legendary outlaw?
9	In what year did pubs in Carlisle fall under the State Management Scheme?
10	At 1483ft above sea level, what is the highest pub in Cumbria?

QUIZ 20

NAME THE TOWN
Can you identify the Cumbrian town from the picture?

ANSWERS
QUIZ 18

1

'In The Sunshine' by Hefin Owen, used under CC BY

2

by Simon Cotterill, used under CC BY

3

'Moot Hall' by summonedbyfells, used under CC BY

1	Torpenhow
2	Head
3	Maryport
4	River Caldew
5	4
6	Buttermere
7	Keswick
8	Sedbergh
9	Westmorland
10	It stands at the mouth of the River Cocker

4

5

6

7

8

9

10

ANSWERS	
QUIZ 19	

INDUSTRY
How much do you know about these businesses in Cumbria?

QUIZ **21**

#	Answer
1	JD Wetherspoon
2	Midland Bank
3	Whitehaven
4	Harry Redfern
5	The Legend Of Oily Johnnies
6	Arms
7	Kendal
8	Robin Hood
9	1916
10	Kirkstone Pass Inn

1	What is the name of the packaging and labelling plant based in Wigton?
2	Tempur Sealy own a factory that manufactures bedding in which Cumbrian town?
3	Which Kendal company make the paper for the Remembrance Day poppies?
4	Which Cumbrian butchers was first established in 1914?
5	Which ironmongers shop has been in Cockermouth since 1836, the deeds for which even feature a signature from William Wordsworth's father?
6	Which company that made miniature handmade models of cottages and scenes was based in Penrith before operations were relocated to Langholm in 2009?
7	Which chain of kitchenware stores has its base in Windermere?
8	Highlighting where they were made, what did the K stand for in K Shoes?
9	Which bakery business was established in Lazonby in 1946?
10	Which food manufacturing company own the Cumbrian-based Eden Valley Mineral Water plant?

	DIALLING CODES			ANSWERS QUIZ 20
1	01900?		1	Alston
2	01228?		2	Ulverston
3	017687?		3	Brampton
4	012293?		4	Penrith
5	015395?		5	Whitehaven
6	016973?		6	Kendal
7	017683?		7	Wigton
8	01946?		8	Keswick
9	012295?		9	Workington
10	015396?		10	Barrow-in-Furness

YEARS (1)
What years did these things happen?

#	Answer
1	Innovia Films
2	Aspatria
3	James Cropper PLC
4	Cranston's
5	J.B. Banks & Son Ltd.
6	Lilliput Lane
7	Lakeland
8	Kendal
9	Bells Of Lazonby
10	Princes

1	The county of Cumbria was formed?
2	South Lakes Wild Animal Park opened?
3	The first Carlisle Fire Show was held in Bitts Park?
4	Carlisle United first played at Wembley?
5	The building of Carlisle Market Hall was completed?
6	The Queen Elizabeth Grammar School in Penrith was established?
7	The Ulverston canal ceased business?
8	The final Cumbrian Woolworths stores in Kendal, Maryport and Barrow-in-Furness closed?
9	The first of Alfred Wainwright's pictorial guides to the Lakeland fells was published?
10	Radio station CFM launched?

1	The tramway in Carlisle closed?
2	Whitehaven became the first place to switch off analogue TV in the UK?
3	Haig Colliery closed, ending mining in Whitehaven?
4	Border Television began broadcasting?
5	Roxanne Pallet walked from Celebrity Big Brother?
6	The Sands Centre in Carlisle opened its doors to the public for the first time?
7	The first edition of William Wordsworth's 'Guide To The Lakes' was published anonymously?
8	Carlisle United topped the English Football League?
9	The IBIS Hotel opened on Botchergate in Carlisle?
10	The first Whitehaven Festival took place?

#	Answer
1	Workington
2	Carlisle
3	Keswick
4	Millom
5	Grange-over-Sands
6	Wigton
7	Appleby
8	Whitehaven
9	Barrow-in-Furness
10	Sedbergh

YEARS (3)
What years did these things happen?

1	1974
2	1994
3	1987
4	1995
5	1889
6	1564
7	1945
8	2009
9	1955
10	1993

1	Debenhams opened in The Lanes Shopping Centre?
2	911 had a top 3 hit with 'Bodyshakin'?
3	The first Cumberland County Show was held?
4	Carlisle United was founded?
5	Portland Walk Shopping Centre opened in Barrow-in-Furness?
6	Many parts of Cumbria flooded as a result of Storm Desmond?
7	A fire broke out at the Windscale facility?
8	A Carlisle edition of the board game Monopoly was released?
9	Train operating company Avanti West Coast took over management of Carlisle railway station?
10	Carlisle Canal was closed and drained?

#	Question	#	Answer
1	The first Great North Swim took place at Windermere?	1	1931
2	Kendal's K Shoes factory was closed?	2	2007
3	Carlisle city centre was pedestrianised?	3	1986
4	Helen Skelton became a *Blue Peter* presenter?	4	1961
5	Barrow became the first football club to win the FA Trophy at both the old and new Wembley Stadium?	5	2018
6	The Lake District National Park was established?	6	1985
7	The building of Carlisle's Civic Centre was completed?	7	1810
8	Primark opened in Carlisle?	8	1974
9	The first Egremont Crab Fair took place?	9	2003
10	Matt Pagan won Britain's Got Talent with Collabro?	10	1999

FUN TIMES

The places where residents and visitors pass the time

QUIZ **27**

1	2000
2	1997
3	1832
4	1904
5	1994
6	2015
7	1957
8	2007
9	2019
10	1853

1	What was the name of Carlisle's Hollywood Bowl before it reverted to its original name in 2020?
2	In which Cumbrian shopping centre would you find the Plaza Cinema?
3	Puddle Lane, Funtastic and Big Softies were all once what kind of attraction in Cumbria?
4	Which animal park is located near Bassenthwaite Lake?
5	Which go-karting centre is in Maryport?
6	There are Go Ape adventure centres at Grizedale and which other Cumbrian forest?
7	Bowness-on -Windermere is the home of a visitor attraction dedicated to which author?
8	Which Carlisle cinema was closed after 75 years in 2006?
9	What was the name of the holiday village situated in Whinfell Forest before being taken over by Center Parcs in 2001?
10	Which laser tag centre first opened in Carlisle in 1993?

#	Question		Answer
1	Which Cumbria news website was run by Carl Fallowfield until it was sold to Barrnon Media in 2020?	1	2008
2	What was the name of the free newspaper with east and west editions delivered weekly to homes?	2	2003
3	What was the first song played on CFM when it launched in April 1993?	3	1989
4	What is the name of the community radio station based in Penrith?	4	2008
5	A free local newspaper called Grange Now serves homes in and around which Cumbrian town?	5	2010
6	What kind of bird did the News & Star use as part of its logo for many years?	6	1951
7	What was the name of BBC Radio Cumbria before it changed its name in May 1982?	7	1964
8	Which Kendal based radio station became Smooth Radio in 2018 after being bought by media group Global?	8	2016
9	Which Carlisle magazine hosts an annual awards celebrating the best businesses in the city?	9	1267
10	Which weekly independent Penrith newspaper has been published since 1860?	10	2014

ANSWERS	
QUIZ 27	

CUMBRIAN DIALECT (1)
Cumbria has its own words and
phrases, but can you translate?

QUIZ
29

1	AMF Bowling
2	Dunmail Park
3	Kids' soft play
4	The Lake District Wildlife Park
5	West Coast Indoor Karting
6	Whinlatter
7	Beatrix Potter
8	Lonsdale Cinema
9	Oasis Holiday Village
10	Lazer Quest

1	'Border Crack-and-deekabout' refers to which TV show?
2	If a Cumbrian referred to 'lowie', what would they be talking about?
3	What Cumbrian word beginning with 'S' is used when something is embarrassing or unfair?
4	If you were charged a 'bar' for something, how much would that be?
5	What part of the body is the 'fizzog'?
6	If a Cumbrian were to 'grotch', what would they be doing?
7	If you had a lot of 'peeve' what would you have plenty of?
8	What would a Cumbrian be doing if they were to 'ratch' for something?
9	If you were to 'nash', what would you be doing?
10	If a Cumbrian asked you to keep your 'neb' out, what would they be asking you to keep out?

QUIZ
30

CUMBRIAN DIALECT (2)
More Cumbrian words to translate
from or to

ANSWERS
QUIZ 28

1	In Cumbrian dialect 'chuddy' refers to what?	1	Cumbria Crack
2	If a Cumbrian asked to pagger with you, what would that mean?	2	Cumbrian Gazette
3	What would a Cumbrian person be doing if they were made to 'bowk'?	3	'The Best' by Tina Turner
4	What article of clothing would you be wearing if you had 'dookers' on?	4	Eden FM
5	If you were a West Cumbrian's 'marra', what would you be to them?	5	Grange-over-sands
6	What would you be having if you were going for some 'scran'?	6	Eagle
7	Where would a Cumbrian be going if they were 'gan yam'?	7	BBC Radio Carlisle
8	What Cumbrian word beginning with 'y' is another way of saying 'one'?	8	Lakeland Radio
9	What part of the body is the 'napper'?	9	Carlisle Living
10	What would be meant by something being described as 'clarty'?	10	The Cumberland & Westmorland Herald

ANSWERS	
QUIZ 29	

1	*Lookaround*
2	Money
3	Shan
4	£1
5	Face
6	Spit
7	Alcoholic beverages
8	Search
9	Running
10	Nose

NIGHT LIFE

All about some of Cumbria's best-loved bars and clubs

QUIZ 31

1	In which Cumbrian town were Blues and Toppers popular nightclubs?
2	What nightspot did Buskers in Carlisle become after it closed in 2004?
3	The building of which former Workington nightclub was destroyed by fire in May 2020?
4	The Blue Lagoon was a nightclub on which ship docked at Barrow-in-Furness in the 2000s?
5	Which Carlisle nightspot was well-known for having telephones on the tables?
6	What was the name of the Carlisle nightclub that opened its doors on West Walls in 2002?
7	After welcoming clubbers throughout the 80s and 90s, what nightspot did the Pagoda become in 2000?
8	In which Cumbrian town was The Park nightclub a popular venue until the mid-noughties?
9	Which Carlisle nightspot was originally named 'The Pink Panther' when it first opened in 1970?
10	Between being The Malt Shovel and Ristorante Adriano, what was the Rickergate location known as?

1	In which Cumbrian town would you find Lakes College?	**1**	Chewing gum
2	Which Cumbrian school formed from the amalgamation of Carlisle Grammar School, The Margaret Sewell School and The Creighton School?	**2**	Fight
3	Which Appleby Grammar School attendee became a Blue Peter presenter in 2008?	**3**	Vomiting
4	Which school merged with the North Cumbria Technology College to become Richard Rose Central Academy in 2008?	**4**	Swimming trunks
5	Comedy actor Rowan Atkinson attended which Cumbrian school?	**5**	Mate/friend
6	Which Queen gives her name to an academy school in Kendal?	**6**	Food
7	Which secondary school is located in the town of Brampton?	**7**	Home
8	In which city is the University of Cumbria's furthest campus from its headquarters in Carlisle?	**8**	Yan
9	In which town is Walney School?	**9**	Head
10	Which TV and movie actor studied at Cumbria College Of Art and Design and was expelled from Queen Elizabeth Grammar School in Penrith?	**10**	Dirty/mucky

FESTIVALS
Cumbria is home to many festival events

QUIZ 33

1	Penrith
2	The Village
3	Fusion
4	Princess Selandia
5	Micks 2
6	Club XS
7	Freedom
8	Whitehaven
9	The Twisted Wheel
10	Hoppers

1	At which Cumbrian festival was a record set for the largest gathering of people dressed as Superman in 2013?
2	The Taste Cumbria food festival is held in which town on the last weekend of September each year?
3	Which two Cumbrian towns beginning with 'K' hold annual mountain festivals?
4	The Osprey Short Film Awards are a part of which Cumbrian film festival?
5	Each year Solfest takes place at Tarnside Farm near which town?
6	Which charity festival sees people gathering to light up fells in the Lake District?
7	A festival dedicated to which fruit preserve takes place annually at Dalemain House near Penrith?
8	Which festival held each August in Penrith is made up of tribute acts?
9	What is the name of the Cockermouth festival that celebrates all things wool?
10	Which summer health and fitness festival first took place at Kirkoswald in 2019?

1	Cumbria's only independently run motorway services is located near which village?
2	Which village's name sign has the words "please dance" printed where "please drive carefully" is often read?
3	Which village is also known as Holme Abbey and gets its name from Holmcultram Abbey?
4	In which Cumbrian village was mutineer Fletcher Christian born?
5	Which village's train station is on the West Coast Main Line?
6	Eden Valley Woollen Mill can be found in which village?
7	Which Cumbrian village was the home of the UK's first website design company in 1996?
8	Which South Cumbrian village contained a factory that produced blue dye for fabrics in an old mill and is also the home of the Lakeland Motor Museum?
9	What is the only pub in the village of Crosby called?
10	Retail chain Klondyke & Strikes have a garden centre near which Cumbrian village?

Answers Quiz 32

#	Answer
1	Workington
2	Trinity School
3	Helen Skelton
4	St Aidan's County High School
5	St Bees School
6	Queen Katherine
7	William Howard School
8	London
9	Barrow-in-Furness
10	Charlie Hunnam

VENUES

Cumbria has many homes of entertainment

QUIZ
35

1	Kendal Calling
2	Cockermouth
3	Keswick and Kendal
4	Keswick Film Festival
5	Silloth
6	Lakeland Festival Of Light
7	Marmalade
8	Wannasee Festival
9	Woolfest
10	Eden Escape Festival

1	Which arts and entertainment venue in Carlisle was formerly the base for an emergency service?
2	Which theatre was built by Workington Town Council and opened in 1904?
3	Which amateur theatre is situated at West Walls in Carlisle?
4	Which theatre opened on the shores of Derwentwater in 1999?
5	What theatre is located on Duke Street in Barrow-in-Furness?
6	In which decade did Her Majesty's Theatre on Lowther Street, Carlisle close, soon after it was renamed Municipal Theatre?
7	Which entertainment venue is the host of the annual Kendal Mountain Festival?
8	By what name is Whitehaven's Civic Hall now known?
9	In which town is The Kirkgate Centre?
10	Until redevelopment in the early 2020s, which Carlisle venue had a seating capacity of 1,400 in its main hall?

QUIZ 36

SELLAFIELD
It's one of Cumbria's best-known places, but how much do you know?

ANSWERS
QUIZ 34

#	Question		Answer
1	To which village is the Sellafield site closest?	1	Tebay
2	The Sellafield Visitor Centre closed in 2008. The history of Sellafield is now exhibited at which tourist attraction in Whitehaven?	2	Castle Carrock
3	What was the name of the world's first commercial nuclear power station situated on the site?	3	Abbeytown
4	Which Cumbrian town was the first in the world to receive electricity produced by nuclear power?	4	Eaglesfield
5	How many square miles does Sellafield cover?	5	Oxenholme
6	Which German electronic band namecheck Sellafield in their 1991 hit 'Radioactivity'?	6	Ainstable
7	What is the name of Sellafield's largest building where commercial nuclear reprocessing came to an end in 2018?	7	Milnthorpe (Big Fish Internet)
8	Which Royal officially opened the Calder Hall nuclear power station in 1956?	8	Backbarrow
9	In which year did a fire at the site cause an emission of radioactive materials?	9	The Stag Inn
10	What was the name of the nuclear energy company who owned Sellafield until 2005?	10	Houghton

POT LUCK (1)
Random questions about Cumbria

QUIZ 37

#	Answer	#	Question
1	Old Fire Station	1	Which Cumbrian cricket club play their home games at the Sandair Ground?
2	Carnegie Theatre	2	What happened at Carlisle's McVities factory to cause a national shortage of ginger nuts, custard creams and bourbons in 2016?
3	Carlisle Green Room Club	3	Which actor, who lived near Penrith as a teenager, once described it as "just about the worst place you could hope to live"?
4	Theatre By The Lake	4	What Cumbrian food was reportedly created accidentally by Joseph Wiper in 1869?
5	The Forum	5	What animal appears on Carlisle's Market Cross?
6	1960s (1963)	6	Where was the Cumberland Show held from 2010 until 2016?
7	The Brewery Arts Centre	7	The children of Kirkby Lonsdale-born Arthur Llewelyn Davies were the inspiration for which stories by J.M. Barrie?
8	The Solway Hall	8	What was the name of the Grange-over-Sands public swimming pool that opened in 2003 only to close 3 years later?
9	Cockermouth	9	In which Cumbrian town would you find the Devil's Bridge?
10	The Sands Centre	10	How was Wigton's Market Cross destroyed during celebrations of Nelson's victory at the Battle of Trafalgar?

1	Carlisle, Penrith, Whitehaven, Great Clifton, Kendal and Flimby all contain a street with the same name beginning with L, what is it?	1	Seascale
2	In which country is Flemsburg, a town that Carlisle is twinned with?	2	The Beacon Museum
3	Which Cumbrian town shares its name with a city in New South Wales, Australia?	3	Calder Hall
4	What major change was made to Carlisle's English Street and Scotch Street in 1989?	4	Workington
5	There are two different two letter combinations that begin postcodes in Cumbria, what are they?	5	2
6	An image of what figure that interested ufologists was said to have been captured in a photo taken by Jim Templeton on Burgh Marsh in 1964?	6	Kraftwerk
7	Where in Cumbria was made an honorary Quidditch town after having a fictitious team named after it in JK Rowling's 'Quidditch Through The Ages – Illustrated Edition'?	7	Thorp (Thermal Oxide Reprocessing Plant)
8	Which word meaning 'to demand benefit in return for not revealing compromising information about someone' originated in Cumbria?	8	Queen Elizabeth II
9	Which Scottish novelist and poet was married at Carlisle Cathedral in 1797?	9	1957
10	The last time England was invaded from the sea was by men led by Captain John Paul Jones at which town?	10	BNFL

POT LUCK (3)
Random questions about Cumbria

QUIZ
39

#	Answer
1	Cockermouth
2	It flooded in December 2015
3	Charlie Hunnam
4	Kendal Mint Cake
5	Lion
6	Carlisle Racecourse
7	Peter Pan
8	Berners Pool
9	Kirkby Lonsdale
10	It was set on fire

1	Which former hamlet that was submerged in water becomes visible again when water levels are low at Haweswater Reservoir?
2	In 2020, climate change activists protested plans to build what in Whitehaven?
3	Which American president's grandmother is buried in Whitehaven?
4	Which TV game show, most recently hosted by Philip Schofield, was filmed in Carlisle in the 70s and 80s?
5	What, in Carlisle, moved from the Swifts to Blackwell in 1904?
6	An 80s TV advert claimed that what sweets were "chewier than Barrow-in-Furness bus depot"?
7	What was the name of the hospital radio based at the Cumberland Infirmary until 2017?
8	Which Carlisle-born writer wrote the book *Diana, Princess Of Wales: How Sexual Politics Shook The Monarchy*?
9	The Coast to Coast (or Sea to Sea) cycle route runs to the north east of England from one of which two Cumbrian towns?
10	In which town are the headquarters of Cumbria Police?

1	Wainwright's beer is named after which fell walker and guidebook author?	**1**	Lowther Street
2	Margaret Forster, writer of the novel *Georgy Girl*, was born in which suburb of Carlisle?	**2**	Germany
3	Which English King died at Burgh-by-Sands in 1307?	**3**	Penrith
4	In which village is the Great North Air Ambulance helicopter 'The Pride of Cumbria' based?	**4**	They were pedestrianised
5	Which charity run, in aid of Cancer Research, took place for the first time at Carlisle in 1998?	**5**	CA and LA
6	Which DIY store filmed a TV commercial at Carlisle Train Station in 2010?	**6**	A Spaceman (the Solway Firth Spaceman)
7	Which pub at Ruleholme closed in 2018 to make way for a multi-million-pound hotel development?	**7**	Appleby
8	What caused the traditional horse race The Carlisle Bell to be run at Thirsk instead of Carlisle in 2001?	**8**	Blackmail
9	Radio 1's Big Weekend at Carlisle in 2011 saw The Foo Fighters headline Saturday's main stage, who headlined on the Sunday?	**9**	Sir Walter Scott
10	Which independent Carlisle record store, run by Keith Jefferson for many years, closed in 2003?	**10**	Whitehaven

POT LUCK (5)
Random questions about Cumbria

QUIZ 41

1	Mardale Green
2	A coal mine
3	George Washington
4	Mr & Mrs
5	Carlisle Racecourse
6	Chewits
7	Radio Echo
8	Beatrix Campbell
9	Whitehaven and Workington
10	Penrith

1	A 2015 TV advert claimed that a man called Ben was "born in Carlisle, but made..." where?
2	Who is the champion fell runner who completed 72 Lake District peaks, over a distance of 100 miles, in under 24 hours?
3	Which Cleator Moor-born footballer has been the goalkeeping coach for Hartlepool United, Bury and Livingston?
4	In the common abbreviation for the Penrith secondary school, what does QEGS stand for?
5	Which Carlisle hospital closed when its services were transferred to the Cumberland Infirmary in 1999?
6	Which Carlisle-educated broadcaster and author was the chairman of BBC Radio 4's *Gardener's Question Time* for over 25 years?
7	What is the name of the former rally driver whose M-Sport team is based at Dovenby Hall near Cockermouth?
8	Cumbria-born Adrian Johnston composed the original score for which 2007 film about Jane Austen?
9	Which Carlisle hotel boasts the only 'glistening wood sprung' dance floor in Cumbria?
10	Newsreader Anna Ford was a head girl at White House Grammar School which existed in which town until 1980?

EMOJIS

Can you identify the Cumbrian place names from these emojis?

ANSWERS QUIZ 40

#	Emojis
1	😇 🐝 🐝
2	🐓 👱‍♀️ 👄
3	🐄 🐄 🏠
4	🌉 🦶
5	🍎 🐝
6	🚗 🚦
7	🌊 ♎
8	🐱 🏛
9	🍷 ➕ 🐝
10	➖ 🏠

#	Answer
1	Alfred Wainwright
2	Raffles
3	Edward I
4	Langwathby
5	Race For Life
6	Homebase
7	The Golden Fleece
8	Foot & Mouth
9	Lady Gaga
10	Pink Panther Records

CARLISLE STREETS

10 questions about the city's streets

QUIZ 43

1	The Royal Navy
2	Joss Naylor
3	Tony Caig
4	Queen Elizabeth Grammar School
5	Carlisle City General/Maternity Hospital
6	Eric Robson
7	Malcolm Wilson
8	*Becoming Jane*
9	The Hallmark Hotel
10	Brampton

1	The Cumberland Infirmary hospital stands on which road?
2	On which Carlisle street would you find Brunton Park football ground?
3	What is the name of the road Carlisle Castle overlooks?
4	The Cumberland Infirmary hospital is on which street?
5	On which street in the city centre would you find a McDonald's, Sports Direct and Poundland?
6	Which primary road has a capital city in its name?
7	What is the name of the steep road that connects Eden Bridge to Stanwix?
8	Which Carlisle street is regularly closed after 9pm on Friday and Saturday to make it safer for those on a night out?
9	Marks & Spencer, House Of Fraser and Clinton Cards can all be found on which street?
10	There are 5 Carlisle roads beginning with the letter Q, can you name one?

QUIZ 44

CUMBRIAN TOWNS
How much do you know about the county's towns?

ANSWERS
QUIZ 42

1	Which Cumbrian town lies within the North Pennines?
2	Which Cumbrian town stands at the mouth of the river Cocker?
3	01539 is the dialling code for which town?
4	The conference, entertainment and exhibition venue The Wave Centre can be found in which town?
5	In which county was Barrow-in-Furness prior to 1974?
6	Which Cumbrian town is twinned with its namesake in Australia?
7	Name all 4 Cumbrian towns that begin with 'W'?
8	Which Cumbrian town hosts the World Gurning Championships every September?
9	Which family built the port that led to the creation of the town of Whitehaven?
10	The name of which Cumbrian town means "at the mills"?

#	Answer
1	St Bees
2	Cockermouth
3	Oxenholme
4	Bridgefoot
5	Appleby
6	Cargo
7	Seascale
8	Catbank
9	Glassonby
10	Ruleholme

RIVERS

Find out how much you know about the rivers in Cumbria

#	Answer	#	Question
1	Newtown Road	1	Cockermouth is situated at the confluence of the River Cocker as it flows into which other river?
2	Warwick Road	2	On which river does Kendal stand?
3	Castle Way	3	Which river destroyed Pooley Bridge during the Storm Desmond floods of 2015?
4	Newtown Road	4	Which Cumbrian river shares its name with a perennial herb?
5	Scotch Street	5	The Devil's Bridge near Kirkby Lonsdale crosses which river?
6	London Road	6	On which river does the town of Alston stand?
7	Stanwix Bank	7	Which river is a tributary of the River Derwent and flows through the town of Keswick?
8	Botchergate	8	Carlisle stands at the confluence of the rivers Eden, Caldew and which other?
9	English Street	9	Which river enters the Irish Sea at the point of Duddon Sands?
10	Quebec Avenue, Queen Street, Queens Drive, Queensway, Quentin Gardens	10	Which river runs through the Sellafield nuclear site?

CFM
Questions on the local commercial
radio station

#	Question
1	As a male known as Jonathan, which CFM newsreader later went on to become Britain's first transgender national television newsreader as a female?
2	Which former Border Television presenter hosted the breakfast show when CFM launched in 1993?
3	What does the 'C' stand for in CFM?
4	In a 2009 CFM competition called *Live In It To Win It*, what did the contestants have to live in for 5 days to win it?
5	Who was the regular host of CFM's *Sunday Night Phone In* until 2003?
6	On what sole FM frequency did CFM broadcast for its first 2 years?
7	Which media company is the current owner of CFM?
8	For which big anniversary did CFM broadcast from as many different places for every year it had been on air in one day?
9	Who has been CFM's breakfast show presenter since 2002?
10	What CFM show, which ran from 2005-2010, was named after a locally produced food?

#	Answer
1	Alston
2	Cockermouth
3	Kendal
4	Maryport
5	Lancashire
6	Penrith
7	Workington, Whitehaven, Windermere and Wigton
8	Egremont
9	Lowther
10	Millom

POPULATIONS

According to the 2011 census, what is the correct population for each?

#	Answer	#	Question
1	Derwent	1	Cockermouth – 8761, 10761 or 12761?
2	River Kent	2	Kendal – 21586, 24586 or 28586?
3	River Eamont	3	Silloth – 1906, 2906 or 3906?
4	River Mint	4	Keswick – 3243, 5243 or 7243?
5	River Lune	5	Brampton – 4627, 5627 or 6627?
6	River Tyne	6	Barrow-in-Furness – 46745, 56745 or 66745?
7	River Greta	7	Workington – 15207, 20207 or 25207?
8	Petteril	8	Ulverston – 11678, 13678 or 15678?
9	River Duddon	9	Bowness-on-Windermere – 3814, 4814 or 5814?
10	River Calder	10	Whitehaven – 19986, 23986 or 27986?

#	Question	#	Answer
1	Which town is the home of Hartley's Ice Cream?	1	India Willoughby
2	Which Michelin-starred Cartmel restaurant is run by chef Simon Rogan?	2	John Myers
3	Betulla's in Ulverston, La Mezzaluna in Carlisle and Villa Bianca in Penrith specialise in which country's cuisine?	3	Carlisle
4	Which dining pub in the village of Skelton was the only eating establishment in Cumbria to be awarded a Michelin Bib Gourmand in 2020?	4	A conservatory
5	Which Ambleside bistro can be found in the cellar of a building where William Wordsworth worked as a distributor of stamps?	5	Mike Charlton
6	What Italian restaurant is situated at Carlisle's Guildhall?	6	96.4
7	Sheep Poo ice cream features on the menu at Brough Castle Ice Cream Parlour & Tearoom in Kirkby Stephen, but what is the 'poo' really?	7	Bauer Media Group
8	Which restaurant chain took over the unit in Carlisle that used to be occupied by nightspots Ba Lo Go and Bar Suede?	8	25th
9	Michelin star-awarded restaurant The Cottage In The Wood can be found by which forest?	9	Robbie Dee
10	The Viceroy in Carlisle, Paprika in Workington and Monsoons in Bowness-on-Windermere specialise in which country's cuisine?	10	*The Cumberland Sausage Show*

MUSIC
Cumbrian musicians and music events in the county

1	8761	**1**	Which band from Egremont had an 80s hit with the song 'Calling All The Heroes'?
2	28586	**2**	Which international music star played a concert at Carlisle's Bitts Park, the night before the Little Mix gig in 2017?
3	2906	**3**	At which Carlisle venue did Elton John perform in 2007?
4	5243	**4**	'A Little Bit More' was a 1999 number 1 hit for which boyband with a Carlisle-born lead singer?
5	4627	**5**	Brampton-born producer Jez Willis is one half of which dance music duo that scored top 10 hits with 'What Can You Do For Me', 'Something Good' and 'Believe In Me' in the 90s?
6	56745	**6**	Which Whitehaven-born songwriter co-composed Cher's 1998 number 1 'Believe'?
7	25207	**7**	Which duo had an indie chart hit in 1995 with 'Blue Army' in celebration of Carlisle United reaching Wembley in the Auto Windscreens Shield?
8	11678	**8**	Which Carlisle-born singer had a top 5 hit in 1995 with 'Total Eclipse Of The Heart' and represented the UK in the 2000 Eurovision Song Contest?
9	3814	**9**	Which Carlisle choir boy reached the final of 'Britain's Got Talent' and scored a top 5 album with 'One Voice'?
10	23986	**10**	Which girl band's scheduled 2nd concert at Bitts Park did not happen in the summer of 2020 due to the coronavirus pandemic?

#	Question	#	Answer
1	Which castle is said to be haunted by the spirit of Tom Fool?	1	Egremont
2	Which hotel's 'Handyman' ghost was investigated in a 2005 episode of the TV show 'Most Haunted'?	2	L'Enclume
3	Which Devonshire Street pub in Carlisle was once a monastery building and noises have reportedly been heard coming from the disued tunnels beneath?	3	Italy
4	The ghost of a woman called Ruth supposedly haunts which inn on the road linking Windermere and Patterdale?	4	The Dog And Gun Inn
5	At which castle was the skeleton of a woman dressed in tartan discovered bricked up in the 19th Century, a lady whose ghost people have said they have seen there?	5	The Old Stamp House
6	Which Brampton pub is said to be haunted by the ghost of Maggie Stobart?	6	Franco's
7	Which hall in Kendal was said to be cursed by a gypsy woman who was turned away and is where the ghosts of a grey lady, a pink lady and a black door have been sighted?	7	Chocolate raisins
8	Balls of light have reportedly been seen dancing over which stone circle located near Keswick?	8	Nando's
9	Which Penrith hotel removed the mirrors in the bar due to many guests reportedly seeing apparitions in them?	9	Whinlatter Forest
10	In which village would you find Moresby Hall which is where numerous skeletal remains have been discovered and is reportedly haunted by ghosts?	10	India

1	It Bites
2	Bryan Adams
3	Brunton Park
4	911
5	Utah Saints
6	Brian Higgins
7	So What
8	Nicki French
9	Andrew Johnston
10	Little Mix

1	What is longer: Hadrian's Wall or the Settle-Carlisle railway?
2	Which mountain's peak is higher: Skiddaw or Helvellyn?
3	What is longer: Cumbria's coastline or the entire M6?
4	The area of which lake is larger: Derwentwater or Coniston Water?
5	Which town has the greater population: Penrith or Ulverston?
6	Which communication mast is taller: Sandale Mast at Wigton or Anthorn radio station?
7	Which theatre has the greater seating capacity: Rosehill Theatre in Whitehaven or Carnegie Theatre in Workington?
8	What is further south: Grange-over-Sands or Kirkby Lonsdale?
9	Which school has the greater enrolment: West Lakes Academy in Egremont or Queen Elizabeth Grammar School in Penrith?
10	Which racecourse is longer: Carlisle or Cartmel?

#	How do you pronounce...?	#	Answers Quiz 50
1	Torpenhowe?	1	Muncaster Castle
2	Beckermet?	2	Dalston Hall
3	Gilcrux?	3	The Thin White Duke
4	Kirkby Stephen?	4	The Kirkstone Pass Inn
5	Distington?	5	Carlisle Castle
6	Keswick?	6	The Blacksmiths Arms
7	Burgh-by-Sands?	7	Levens Hall
8	Brougham?	8	Castlerigg Stone Circle
9	Broughton Moor?	9	Edenhall Country Hotel
10	Houghton?	10	Parton

CUMBRIAN CHARACTERS

Mascots, characters and legends of Cumbria

QUIZ 53

1	Hadrian's Wall (by 1 mile)
2	Helvellyn (by 19 metres)
3	The M6 (by 52 miles)
4	Derwentwater (by 0.17 square miles)
5	Penrith (by about 3500)
6	Anthorn radio station (by 74 metres)
7	Carnegie Theatre (by 98 seats)
8	Grange-over-Sands
9	West Lakes Academy (by 332)
10	Carlisle (by 3 furlongs)

1	The name of Carlisle United's fox mascot is an anagram of which football-related word?
2	What is the name of Eddie Stobart's cartoon mascot?
3	By what title was prophetess Mary Baynes known around the Tebay area in the 18th Century?
4	What was the name of the postman with a black and white cat who was created by a Kendal primary school teacher?
5	Which animal character might kids write a letter to at Tullie House Museum in Carlisle?
6	In 2009, the Eden Valley Hospice's mascot Joe Jigsaw was replaced by a cat named what?
7	Which Cumbrian castle is believed to be the only historic home in the UK to still appoint an official Fool?
8	What is the name of the mascot of the Cumbria School Games?
9	At which visitors centre in Cumbria did a character called 'The Mighty Atom' tell the story of recycling spent fuel?
10	Which sheep character is the face of a Lake District gift and homeware brand based in Kendal?

QUIZ 54	**CRYPTIC PLACE NAMES (1)** All places in Cumbria, but can you decrypt the names?	**ANSWERS QUIZ 52**

1	Blemish Ignite	**1**	Tra-pen-ah
2	L.S. Mound	**2**	Buh-kerr-met
3	Bing Black Bird's Value	**3**	Gill-crooz (with a hard 'g')
4	Winton Prime	**4**	Kerr-bee Stee-ven
5	Meander Edge	**5**	Diss-ing-tun
6	Willoughby Timber Basin	**6**	Kezz-ick
7	Solid Candle Cord Big Top	**7**	Bruff-by-sands
8	Conversing Lake	**8**	Broom
9	Middle Greens	**9**	Bror-tun Moor
10	Perk Up An Oral Cavity	**10**	How-tun

CRYPTIC PLACE NAMES (2)

All places in Cumbria, but can you decrypt the names?

QUIZ 55

1	Goal (Olga)
2	Steady Eddie
3	The Witch Of Tebay
4	Postman Pat
5	Tullie Mouse
6	Hospuss
7	Muncaster Castle
8	Spirit
9	Sellafield Visitors Centre
10	Herdy

1	Paddle Weight
2	Black Bird Window
3	Brew Cove
4	Prickle Mound
5	The Avenues
6	Bacardi Tale
7	Fumble A Garden Entrance
8	Bumble Metallic Container
9	William's Dwelling
10	Moggie Chimes

QUIZ
56

CRYPTIC PLACE NAMES (3)
All places in Cumbria, but can you
decrypt the names?

ANSWERS
QUIZ 54

1	The Clooney Inn	1	Stainburn
2	Excellent Centre Drone	2	Lowry Hill
3	Fragments Position Car	3	Crosby Ravensworth
4	Overshadow Recreation	4	Dalemain
5	Get By Touch Down	5	Ambleside
6	Pale Retreat	6	Hollywood Bowl
7	Good Person Bumbles	7	Hardwicke Circus
8	Move Outside	8	Talkin Tarn
9	Whisky Road	9	Center Parcs
10	Hand-Pushed Vehicle On Fire	10	Cockermouth

CRYPTIC PLACE NAMES (4)

All places in Cumbria, but can you decrypt the names?

	Answers Quiz 55			Quiz 57
1	Orton		1	Employed One Hundred
2	Ravenglass		2	Dark Escort
3	Tebay		3	Small Automobile
4	Thornhill		4	Anorak Mound
5	The Lanes		5	Angry Garden Entrances
6	Rum Story		6	Approach Dale
7	Botchergate		7	Ginger Prince Drone
8	Beacon		8	Monarch Dock
9	Wordsworth House		9	Chilling Atop A Drone
10	Catbells		10	Berry Harbour

CRYPTIC PLACE NAMES (5)

All places in Cumbria, but can you decrypt the names?

ANSWERS QUIZ 56

#	Clue		#	Answer
1	The Conjury Fortress		1	The George Hotel
2	Calvin's Playground		2	Great Corby
3	Posh Spice's Bridge Of Arches		3	Bitts Park
4	People Of England's Road		4	Eclipse Leisure
5	Mother's Aquatic Creature Eatery		5	Copeland
6	Not Old Not Small Not Out		6	Whitehaven
7	Dark Water Hole		7	St Bees
8	Apple Middle Buzzing Insect Mound		8	Go Outdoors
9	Not Less One Hundred		9	Scotch Street
10	Dock Line		10	Barrow-In-Furness

CRYPTIC PLACE NAMES (6)

All places in Cumbria, but can you decrypt the names?

QUIZ 59

	Answers Quiz 57
1	Workington
2	Blackford
3	Carlisle
4	Cotehill
5	Crossgates
6	Cumwhinton
7	Harraby
8	Kingmoor
9	Lazonby
10	Maryport

	Quiz 59
1	The City's Harbour
2	Purple Fruit Touch Down
3	Endure Everything
4	Opposite North Pause
5	Pot Apartments
6	Woolly Flock Get On Top
7	Ocean Climb
8	Toupee Weight
9	Hire Valley
10	Broadcast A Power

QUIZ 60

CRYPTIC PLACE NAMES (7)
All places in Cumbria, but can you decrypt the names?

#	Clue		#	Answer
1	Obstruction Honey-Maker		1	The Magic Castle
2	Blemish Tumbled Fish		2	Harris Park
3	Impact Not Off Playground		3	Victoria Viaduct
4	Farmstead Above The Beach		4	English Street
5	Accomplished Man Puts Car Into Position		5	Mamma's Fish Restaurant
6	Green For Sale		6	Newbiggin
7	Spanish Sun Route Darcy Colin		7	Blackwell
8	Laurel Arrests NatWest		8	Corby Hill
9	Window Not Off		9	Morton
10	The Honey Maker Cheat		10	Moor Row

WHERE IN CARLISLE?

Little bits of places in Carlisle's city centre, but where are they?

1	Port Carlisle
2	Plumbland
3	Wetheral
4	Southwaite
5	Clay Flatts
6	Sheepmount
7	Seascale
8	Wigton
9	Borrowdale
10	Aira Force

1

2

3

4

5

6

7

1	Walby
2	Scafell Pike
3	Brunton Park
4	Grange-over-Sands
5	Dunmail Park
6	Sellafield
7	Solway Firth
8	Stanwix Bank
9	Glasson
10	The Beacon

8

9

10

DID YOU KNOW...?

There is a Whitehaven cheese, but it's nothing to do with Whitehaven in Cumbria. It's a goat's milk cheese made in Cheshire!

One of Helen Skelton's early broadcasting jobs was working in the newsroom at CFM.

The weather station at Styhead Tarn near Borrowdale records the highest average annual rainfall total at 4562mm.

Barrow-in-Furness had it's own commercial radio station in the 2000s. Abbey FM launched in 2006, but was forced to close less than 3 years later after being placed into administration.

Cumbria covers an area of 2,613 square miles.

In 2012 Carlisle was named the happiest city in the UK.

Beatrix Potter left her house in Near Sawrey to the National Trust on the proviso the interior was kept just as she left it.

There are six times more sheep in Cumbria than there are people.

The first pencil was invented after graphite discovered at Seathwaite was used for marking sheep. It was learned that the graphite could be shaped into sticks, thus creating the pencil.

ANSWERS QUIZ 61

1	The Lanes (Globe Lane Entrance)

2	Gallagher's Bar

3	Crown & Mitre Hotel

4	The Griffin

5	House Of Fraser

6	Coco Mill

7	Guildhall Museum

8	Carlisle Train Station

9	The Caledonian

10	Lloyds Bank

ROXANNE PALLETT

A Carlisle actress who has certainly caused waves

1	Which Carlisle secondary school did Roxanne attend?
2	What character did she play in *Emmerdale*?
3	In 2005 she won a celebrity edition of *Stars In Their Eyes* performing as which Cuban-American singer?
4	For which Cumbrian hospice did she raise £70,000 by competing on the ITV singing show *Soapstar Superstar* in 2006?
5	On which Yorkshire radio station was Roxanne the breakfast show co-presenter in 2018?
6	In which BBC TV show did she play schoolgirl Shelby Dixon?
7	Roxanne quit which reality TV show in 2018 following an incident that generated more than 25,000 complaints to Ofcom?
8	In which American city did Roxanne marry Jason Carrion in 2020?
9	What kind of flower does Roxanne Pallet have named after her?
10	With which Britain's Got Talent winner was Roxanne paired when she competed on *Celebrity Coach Trip* in 2019?

1	Anne Woods from Egremont is the world record holder for the most female wins of what competition?	The Eden district of Cumbria is the least densely populated local authority in England.
2	At which adventure centre in Grizedale did 106-year-old Jack Reynolds break the world record for the oldest person to ride a zip wire?	In December 2015 a total of 7,465 properties were flooded in Cumbria.
3	75 volunteers for the Cumbria Cerebral Palsy Society pushed **what** 240 miles to set a world record in 2000?	
4	At which town did 1180 people set a world record for the largest shaving cream pie fight at Another Fine Fest?	Christmas lights used to be displayed along Botchergate in Carlisle depicting the 12 Days
5	Scott Smith and Kim Roberts hold the world record for the most times a team of two throw and go through a back-spinning **what** in 30 seconds, set in Flookburgh?	of Christmas, but after many shops closed, and the street became run down in the 90s, a decision was made to
6	Which Cumbrian charity set a world record for the longest line of pom-poms (29,312) at The Lanes Shopping Centre in 2016?	discontinue the illuminations there.
7	At which golf driving range did Sean Murphy hit 2146 balls into a target area setting a world record in 1995?	In 1895 Windermere was completely frozen for six weeks meaning visitors could
8	What can Levens Hall in Kendal boast the world's oldest of?	walk right across it.
9	In 2013 867 people set a world record at Kendal Calling for the largest gathering of people dressed as which superhero?	Rum butter is a Cumbrian delicacy and is believed to have originated in the county
10	A team at Whitehaven Sports Centre achieved 711 goals within an hour setting a world record in which sport?	due to rum being imported by ships to Whitehaven, Workington and Maryport in the 18th century.

WHICH TOWN? SCHOOLS
In which town would you find each of these schools?

QUIZ 64

#	Answer
1	Trinity School
2	Jo Stiles/Sugden
3	Gloria Estefan
4	Eden Valley Hospice
5	Minster FM
6	*Waterloo Road*
7	*Celebrity Big Brother*
8	New York
9	A rose (called Rosa Roxanne Pallett)
10	George Sampson

1	The Queen Katherine School?
2	William Howard School?
3	Netherall School?
4	West Lakes Academy?
5	Walney School?
6	Queen Elizabeth Grammar School?
7	St Benedict's Catholic High School?
8	The Lakes School?
9	St Joseph's Roman Catholic High School?
10	The Nelson Thomlinson School?

#	Pub	#	Answer
1	The Board & Elbow?	1	World Gurning Championships
2	The Globe Tavern?	2	Go Ape
3	The Whittington Cat?	3	Wheelchair
4	The Pack Horse Inn?	4	Ulverston
5	The Stan Laurel Inn?	5	Hula hoop
6	The Rifleman's Arms?	6	Eden Valley Hospice
7	The Captain Nelson Tavern?	7	Swifts, Carlisle
8	The Bitter End?	8	Topiary garden
9	The Henry Bessemer?	9	Superman
10	The Nag's Head?	10	Netball

WHICH TOWN? EATERIES

In which town would you find each of these restaurants?

1	Kendal		1	Taste Of Bengal?
2	Brampton		2	Portofinos?
3	Maryport		3	Pedro's Casa?
4	Egremont		4	Zest Harbourside?
5	Barrow-In-Furness		5	Bosun's Locker?
6	Penrith		6	Superfish?
7	Whitehaven		7	Casa Bella?
8	Windermere		8	Hyltons?
9	Workington		9	Misto?
10	Wigton		10	Betulla's?

1	Which TV sitcom was set in a Cumbrian prison?
2	What is the name of the fictional Cumbria village where Postman Pat lives?
3	*Coronation Street* villain Pat Phelan cheated death after falling into the sea at which Cumbrian town?
4	Which BBC TV drama that was filmed in Cumbria aired its third series in 2020 and starred Morven Christie and Christopher Eccleston?
5	David Tattersall, the Director of Photography for the films *The Green Mile*, *Die Another Day* and *Star Wars* Episodes I, II and III, was born in which Cumbrian town?
6	Which film starring Richard E. Grant and Paul McCann was filmed at Sleddale Hall near Shap?
7	John Simm and Emma Cunniffe starred in which 1997 TV drama set in the Lake District and filmed around Patterdale?
8	A house in Coniston was the setting for a fictional B&B in which 2015 ITV drama starring Christopher Eccleston and Marsha Thomason?
9	Longtown-born actor Simon Greenall provides the voice of which comparison site advert character?
10	Derwentwater was used to film lakeside scenes for which Star Wars movie?

#	Answer
1	Penrith
2	Longtown
3	Whitehaven
4	Keswick
5	Ulverston
6	Kendal
7	Maryport
8	Cockermouth
9	Workington
10	Brampton

ANSWERS QUIZ 66

1	Penrith
2	Cockermouth
3	Kendal
4	Whitehaven
5	Barrow-in-Furness
6	Workington
7	Keswick
8	Bowness-on-Windermere
9	Ambleside
10	Ulverston

BEATRIX POTTER

She wrote her famous stories in Cumbria and made it her home

QUIZ 68

1	What kind of animal was Mr Jeremy Fisher?
2	What is the name of Peter Rabbit's mother?
3	In whose garden is Peter Rabbit particularly mischievous?
4	In which Cumbrian town is The World Of Beatrix Potter attraction?
5	Who played Beatrix in the 2006 film Miss Potter?
6	The woods around Graythwaite Hall in Hawkshead were the setting for which book about a guinea pig who runs away to join the circus?
7	What is the name of Beatrix's Lake District house which she left to the National Trust when she died?
8	To whom did Beatrix Potter refuse the rights to make a *Peter Rabbit* feature film in 1936?
9	On which value coin did a series of Beatrix Potter characters appear in 2016?
10	What relation is Benjamin Bunny to Peter Rabbit?

QUIZ
69

CASTLES
How much do you know about the
many fortresses in Cumbria?

**ANSWERS
QUIZ 67**

1	Before ascending to the throne, which English King lived at Penrith Castle?	1	*Porridge*
2	Which King ordered the construction of Carlisle Castle in 1092?	2	Greendale
3	Which village castle overlooking the River Eden is said to be haunted by a ghost known as 'the radiant boy'?	3	Whitehaven
4	Which town's castle was the home of the dowager Lady Egremont until her death in 2003?	4	*The A Word*
5	Which Cumbrian castle has a keep known as Caesar's Tower?	5	Barrow-in-Furness
6	Which castle has a competition to recruit a jester in celebration of the art of tomfoolery?	6	*Withnail & I*
7	The legend of a horn that only the rightful heir of which castle could blow was the subject of a poem by William Wordsworth?	7	*The Lakes*
8	Which Scottish Queen was imprisoned at Carlisle Castle in 1567?	8	*Safe House*
9	The remains of which town's castle lie opposite its railway station?	9	Aleksandr Orlov in the comparethemarket. com adverts
10	Which castle is located on an island just off the southern tip of the Furness peninsula?	10	*Star Wars VII: The Force Awakens*

SUBURBS (1)
Of which places in Cumbria are these suburbs?

QUIZ 70

#	Answer
1	Frog
2	Josephine
3	Mr McGregor
4	Bowness-on-Windermere
5	Renée Zellweger
6	*The Fairy Caravan*
7	Hill Top
8	Walt Disney
9	50p
10	Cousin

1	Ellenborough?
2	Pategill?
3	Chestnut Hill?
4	Salterbeck?
5	Kirkbarrow?
6	Corkickle?
7	Upperby?
8	Outcast?
9	Roose?
10	Goat?

SUBURBS (2)
Of which places in Cumbria are these suburbs?

ANSWERS
QUIZ 69

1	Sandylands?
2	Hensingham?
3	Vickerstown?
4	Station Hill?
5	Harraby?
6	Netherton?
7	Lilyhall?
8	Townhead?
9	Briar Rigg?
10	Croftlands?

1	Richard III
2	William II (William Rufus)
3	Corby Castle
4	Cockermouth
5	Appleby Castle
6	Muncaster Castle
7	Egremont Castle
8	Mary, Queen of Scots
9	Penrith
10	Piel Castle

HELEN SKELTON

How much do you know about the TV presenter from Cumbria?

QUIZ 72

1	Maryport
2	Penrith
3	Keswick
4	Workington
5	Kendal
6	Whitehaven
7	Carlisle
8	Ulverston
9	Barrow-in-Furness
10	Cockermouth

1	Helen became a co-presenter on which radio station's breakfast show in 2005?
2	Helen is qualified as a teacher of what type of dance?
3	In 1999 Helen appeared as an extra on which TV soap?
4	Helen grew up in a farm near which Cumbrian village?
5	In 2008 Helen became the 33rd presenter of which long-running kids TV show?
6	Helen's brother Gavin is a professional in which sport?
7	In 2012 Helen took part in the Christmas special of which TV challenge show?
8	Since 2008 Helen has been a presenter on which rural-focused BBC TV show?
9	In 2010 Helen kayaked the entire length of which river to raise money for Sport Relief?
10	Helen walked a 150-metre tightrope between chimneys at which power station in 2012?

#	Question		Answer
1	Which shop was responsible for the creation of Carlisle Gin in 2018?	1	Kendal
2	Which craft beer brewery is situated in Stavely near Kendal?	2	Whitehaven
3	In the 1970s which Prime Minister brought an end to the State Management of the brewing, distribution and sale of alcohol in and around Carlisle?	3	Barrow-in-Furness
4	Which brewery based at Rowrah brews beer using water from the lake it's named after?	4	Wigton
5	'Fine Line', 'Atomic Theory' and 'Night Vision' are all beers created by which brewery in Cockermouth?	5	Carlisle
6	Which Cumbrian gin was created by husband and wife Andy & Zoe Arnold-Bennett in their shed in Ulverston?	6	Maryport
7	Which whisky distillery is situated on the shore of Bassenthwaite Lake?	7	Workington
8	Which company makes Kendal Mint Cake Liqueur?	8	Penrith
9	What word beginning with 'P' is sometimes used in the Cumbria dialect in place of 'alcohol'?	9	Keswick
10	Which brewers regularly use the word 'thirst' in their beer names since their inaugural 'Thirst Run' in 2006?	10	Ulverston

ANSWERS
QUIZ 72

1	BBC Radio Cumbria
2	Tap dance
3	*Coronation Street*
4	Kirkby Thore
5	*Blue Peter*
6	Football
7	*Strictly Come Dancing*
8	*Countryfile*
9	River Amazon
10	Battersea Power Station

SPORTING VENUES
The places where many have enjoyed sport in the county

1	Apart from Carlisle, where is the only other racecourse in Cumbria?
2	The finish line for the Great Cumbrian Run is at which athletics ground?
3	Which football team play their home games at Holker Street?
4	What is the name of the primary home ground of Cumberland County Cricket Club in Carlisle?
5	What is the name of Whitehaven's rugby league stadium?
6	Which sporting venue has a section that many still refer to as the 'Warwick Road End'?
7	At which stadium was Workington Comets' speedway track prior to withdrawing from racing in 2019?
8	What sport is played at Craven Park in Barrow-in-Furness?
9	Which open-air swimming pool in South Cumbria closed in 1993 after 61 years?
10	Which football team's home ground is Borough Park?

#	Question		Answer
1	Which village is home to Cumbria's only prison?	1	The House Of Malt
2	Cumbria has England's only mountain to stand over 3200 feet above sea level, what is it?	2	Hawkshead Brewery
3	In what century did Cumbria get its only cathedral at Carlisle?	3	Edward Heath
4	Which is the only town in Cumbria to have a higher population than 50,000?	4	Ennerdale Brewery
5	Which forest 5 miles from Keswick is England's only true mountain forest?	5	Jennings
6	What is the only true lake in the Lake District?	6	Shed 1 Gin
7	What is the only lake in England to exceed 5 square miles in area?	7	The Lakes Distillery
8	Where is the only coastal village in the Lake District National Park that was within the county of Cumberland?	8	Pennington's
9	In which decade did Carlisle United spend just one week at the top of the English Football League?	9	Peeve
10	Which motorway services is the only one in Cumbria to be independently-run?	10	Keswick Brewing Company

#	Answer
1	Cartmel
2	The Sheepmount
3	Barrow
4	Edenside
5	Recreation Ground
6	Brunton Park
7	Derwent Park
8	Rugby League
9	Grange Lido
10	Workington

1	What is the land area of Cumbria in kilometres? 6,769, 7,269 or 7,769 sq km?
2	For how many years was Carlisle's ship canal operational in the 19th century: 30, 50 or 70 years?
3	Which one of these Carlisle landmarks was built the earliest: Dixon's Chimney, Carlisle Railway Station or Tullie House?
4	Which one of these Cumbrian towns has the highest population according to the 2011 census: Maryport, Penrith or Workington?
5	Which one of these towns is not in the Allerdale district: Silloth, Aspatria or Millom?
6	Which of these Cumbrian celebrities is the youngest: Helen Skelton, Roxanne Pallet or Matt Pagan?
7	Which one of these towns is the furthest north: Whitehaven, Penrith or Workington?
8	Which of these Cumbrian towns did not appear in some form in the Domesday Book: Ulverston, Workington or Millom?
9	Which of these bodies of water is the largest: Buttermere, Coniston Water or Ullswater?
10	Which one of these Cumbrian towns has the lowest population according to the 2011 census: Cockermouth, Brampton or Wigton?

#	Question		#	Answer
1	What was the pick 'n' mix sweet shop called that shared its name with an insect?		1	Haverigg
2	Which supermarket was opened by Coronation Street actors Ken Morley and Liz Dawn in 1992?		2	Scafell Pike
3	What kind of business was Key Largo?		3	12th
4	Which store selling car parts, camping gear and bicycles moved from The Lanes to bigger premises on London Road?		4	Barrow-in-Furness
5	The entrance to which department store which was popular in the 80s was situated where Superdrug now stands?		5	Whinlatter Forest
6	What was the name of the spa offering fish pedicures that opened in 2011?		6	Bassenthwaite Lake (the others are meres and waters)
7	Originally one of the first to open in 1984, which clothing store disappeared from The Lanes when the chain closed their UK stores at the turn of the century?		7	Windermere
8	Which entertainment store was opened in 1995 and became Zavvi in 2007?		8	Ravenglass
9	What kind of shop was Tandy on Globe Lane?		9	1970s (1974)
10	What 'K' was a restaurant on Lowther Street which opened as part of the Lanes in 1987?		10	Tebay

THE LANES AS IT WAS (2)
More memories of what used to be
in the Lanes Shopping Centre

QUIZ 78

	Answers Quiz 76		Quiz 78 Questions
1	6,769 sq km	1	Statues of what animals could be found at the water feature in the middle of the Lanes?
2	30 years	2	Which Lanes cafe was named after a Charles Dickens character?
3	Dixon's Chimney	3	On which lane would you have visited The Cornish Candy Shoppe?
4	Workington	4	What nightclub opened in 1992 where Lanes Vaults and Fantasy was?
5	Millom	5	Which department store occupied the unit where Primark now stands?
6	Matt Pagan	6	Which 50s American-style diner chain had a restaurant in the Lanes in the 2010s?
7	Penrith	7	What supermarket was a part of the Lanes in the 80s before becoming Gateway?
8	Workington	8	What kind of product did Peter Lord specialise in?
9	Ullswater	9	Which electrical store disappeared from the Lanes in 2005?
10	Brampton	10	What did the store Fosters sell which was situated on Globe Lane?

#	Previous Name	#	Answer
1	Ellenfoot	1	Butterfly
2	Wurcington	2	Food Giant
3	Bulnes	3	Cafe
4	Braunton	4	Halfords
5	Caer-luel	5	County Store
6	Wicga's tūn	6	Yoko Fish Spa
7	Ulurestun	7	C&A
8	Kent dair	8	Virgin Megastore
9	Cēse wic	9	Electronics
10	Hvit hafn	10	Krakatoa

SPORT

Questions on sportspeople, events and achievements

QUIZ 80

	Answers			Questions
1	Otters		1	The earliest record of what sport taking place in England is at Netherby in AD 210?
2	Mr Pickwick's		2	From what material is the ball made that is used in the Uppies and Downies each Easter?
3	Globe Lane		3	Which annual cycling event included Cumbria in its stages for 7 years of the 2010s?
4	Ruby Tuesdays		4	In which West Cumbrian town did cricketer Ben Stokes grow up?
5	BHS		5	Which town's football club play their games at Parkside Road Stadium?
6	Ed's Easy Diner		6	The prize for which horse race run annually at Carlisle is believed to be the oldest horse racing prize in Britain?
7	Fine Fare		7	With which football club did Carlisle-born Peter Thompson win the First Division title in 1964 and 1966?
8	Shoes		8	Which rally driver formed the Cockermouth-based company now known as M-Sport in 1979?
9	Dixons		9	Which Cumbrian rugby league club were crowned League 1 champions in 2020?
10	Clothing		10	Which Carlisle runner represented Great Britain in the 5000m at the 2016 Olympic Games?

#	Question		#	Answer
1	The World Gurning Championships is a feature of which annual Cumbrian fair?		1	Maryport
2	An awards event honouring which food stuff is held at Dalemain House near Penrith each March?		2	Workington
3	The Bridge Inn at Santon Bridge is famous for a contest to find the World's biggest what?		3	Bowness-on-Windermere
4	The actress who played which Coronation Street character switched on Carlisle's Christmas lights in 2000?		4	Brampton
5	The Kendal Calling Festival takes place near which Cumbrian town?		5	Carlisle
6	In which town does the "biggest traditional Gypsy Fair in Europe" take place annually?		6	Wigton
7	Which annual Cumbrian awards include 'Small Visitor Attraction of the Year', 'Wedding Venue of the Year' and 'Large Hotel of the Year'?		7	Ulverston
8	The Cumbria Sausage Festival takes place annually at which venue?		8	Kendal
9	Which festival takes place at Tarnside Farm near Silloth during the August bank holiday weekend?		9	Keswick
10	In which month of the year does the Westmorland County Show take place?		10	Whitehaven

ANSWERS
QUIZ 80

1	Horse racing
2	Cow leather
3	Tour Of Britain
4	Cockermouth
5	Kendal
6	The Carlisle Bell
7	Liverpool
8	Malcolm Wilson
9	Whitehaven
10	Tom Farrell

PUZZLE PLACES (1)

Can you get the Cumbrian place names from the cryptic images?

QUIZ 82

1

A B C

2

FURBARROWNESS

3

HAVEN

4

T O W N

5

cowshed

6

BARBIE &
SINDY'S 100

1	Egremont Crab Fair
2	Marmalade
3	Liar
4	Vera Duckworth (Liz Dawn)
5	Penrith
6	Appleby-in-Westmorland
7	Cumbria Tourism Awards
8	Muncaster Castle
9	Solfest
10	September

7

CAPTAIN JAMES T. LEE HARVEY

8

9

MOOR MOOR MOOR MOOR

10

1

GEORGE WASHINGTON MOOR

GEORGE HARRISON MOOR

GEORGE VI MOOR ⇐

2

KEVIN   BRUCE   ALAN

3

NEBIGW

4

BACON   £2.99
PORK   £2.99
HAM   £99.99

5

MANSION   MANSION

BOLT   BOLT
BUNGALOW   BUNGALOW

6

ONE
THOUSAND
KG

7

C D E F G A B C

8

TOWORKN

9

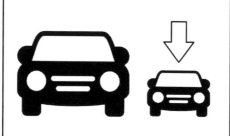

10

BROUGHT
MOOR

BODIES OF WATER

There are a lot of them in Cumbria, but how much do you know?

QUIZ 84

1	Appleby
2	Barrow-in-Furness
3	Whitehaven
4	Longtown
5	Oxenholme
6	Dalston
7	Kirkoswald
8	Dovenby
9	Moor Row
10	Pooley Bridge

1	Peel Island can be found on which body of water in the Lake District?
2	Which body of water at Wasdale is the deepest lake in England?
3	Which reservoir is owned by United Utilities and supplies roughly a quarter of the North West's water supply?
4	Which is the only body of water in the Lake District to have the word 'lake' in its name?
5	What is the second largest lake in the Lake District?
6	Theatre By The Lake stands on the shores of which body of water?
7	Which small lake in the Hartsop valley was known as Broad Water until its name was changed after two brothers drowned there in the 19th century?
8	On which body of water did Donald Campbell lose his life attempting to break the world water speed record?
9	Belle Isle is the largest of 19 islands in which body of water?
10	Which body of water's name means 'the lake by the dairy pastures'?

QUIZ
85

THE M6
All about the motorway that runs
through the county

1	Which services can be accessed southbound between J37 and J36?
2	Which is the most northerly junction of the M6?
3	Heading northbound, what are the first services you would come to within Cumbria?
4	In which decade was the northern end of the M6 extended to make Gretna the terminus?
5	J41 is the exit for which town beginning with 'W'?
6	Between which junctions do the northbound and southbound carriageways split apart?
7	Which services are located between J38 and J39?
8	At which junction would you be exiting at the south end of Carlisle?
9	At which junction is the main exit for Kirkby Lonsdale?
10	At which services could you stop between J41 and J42?

GET FRESH

Guess if the Saturday kids TV show was broadcast from these places

QUIZ 86

1	Coniston Water
2	Wast Water
3	Haweswater
4	Bassenthwaite Lake
5	Ullswater
6	Derwentwater
7	Brothers Water
8	Coniston Water
9	Windermere
10	Buttermere

1	The Glebe, Windermere?
2	Vulcan Park, Workington?
3	Killington Lake Services?
4	Carlisle Castle?
5	Silloth Green?
6	Lowther Castle, Penrith?
7	The Sheepmount Stadium, Carlisle?
8	Whitehaven Harbour?
9	Fitz Park, Keswick?
10	Brunton Park, Carlisle?

QUIZ
87

FRUIT
Random questions about Cumbria
with a fruity connection

**ANSWERS
QUIZ 85**

1	What fruit gets thrown to people in Main Street as part of the Egremont Crab Fair?
2	One of the lanes of the Lanes Shopping Centre in Carlisle shares its name with what fruit?
3	The Lemon Tree Café Bistro can be found at Devonshire Arcade in which town?
4	Which brand created the fruit juice drink Um Bongo in Milnthorpe?
5	An Indian restaurant in Cardewlees, Carlisle until 2020 shared its name with an Indian restaurant in Kirkby Stephen - The *what* tree?
6	What fruit completes the name of the Whitehaven pub: Joe...?
7	Which pub in Barrow-in-Furness shares its name with a fruit?
8	Which health food chain has shops in the Westmorland Shopping Centre in Kendal and The Lanes Shopping Centre in Carlisle?
9	Which village just north of Penrith contains a fruit in its name?
10	Which fruit is missing from the Seascale Italian restaurant The Wild _____, the Cockermouth beauty salon _____ Tree Beauty and the Turkish eatery Café _____ in Kendal?

#	Answer
1	Killington Lake
2	J45
3	Burton-in-Kendal
4	2000s (opened 2008)
5	Wigton
6	J39 and J38
7	Tebay
8	J42
9	J36
10	Southwaite

FELL ANAGRAMS

Quite simply anagrams of fell names to unscramble

QUIZ
88

1	Yes
2	No
3	Yes
4	Yes
5	No
6	No
7	Yes
8	Yes
9	No
10	No

1	Please Flick
2	Elf Bowl
3	Beggar Tale
4	Rip All
5	Ranch Table
6	Shaky Cats
7	Best Call
8	Most Idol Cannon
9	Ideal Riff
10	Cacklers Grin

QUIZ
89

LEE BRENNAN
How much do you know about the
Carlisle-born lead singer of 911?

ANSWERS
QUIZ 87

1	What are the names of Lee's 911 bandmates?	1	Apples
2	At which Carlisle nightspot were 911 officially launched in June 1995?	2	Grapes
3	Lee married a member of which girl group in 2006?	3	Penrith
4	Which Carlisle secondary school did Lee attend?	4	Libby's
5	What was the name of 911's debut album?	5	Mango
6	Which 1999 single gave 911 their only UK number 1?	6	Bananas
7	Of which football team is Lee a fan and wanted to play for?	7	The Strawberry
8	With which Bee Gees-penned song did 911 score a number 2 hit in 1998?	8	Grape Tree
9	911 took part in which ITV2 reality-documentary series in 2013 which followed many reuniting pop bands as they rehearsed for a comeback performance?	9	Plumpton
10	Lee played the Prince in which Sands Centre pantomime production in 2017?	10	Olive

ANSWERS
QUIZ 88

FUNNY NAMES (1)

They're all real place names but are they in Cumbria or not?

	ANSWERS QUIZ 88			FUNNY NAMES (1)
1	Scafell Pike		1	Black Butts Lane?
2	Bowfell		2	Crotch Crescent?
3	Great Gable		3	Trumpet Terrace?
4	Pillar		4	Fanny House Farm?
5	Blencathra		5	Beaver Road?
6	Haystacks		6	Birks Road?
7	Catbells		7	Spanker Lane?
8	Coniston Old Man		8	Backside Lane?
9	Fairfield		9	Finkle Street?
10	Crinkle Crags		10	Trailcock Road?

QUIZ
91

FUNNY NAMES (2)
More real place names but are they
in Cumbria or not?

**ANSWERS
QUIZ 89**

#	Question		#	Answer
1	Knick Knack Lane?		1	Spike & Jimmy
2	Buckle Avenue?		2	The Pagoda
3	Low Bell End Farm?		3	B*Witched (Lindsay)
4	Great Cockup?		4	Newman Catholic School
5	Willie Horne Way?		5	'The Journey'
6	Hooker Road?		6	'A Little Bit More'
7	Cockfield Drive?		7	Carlisle United
8	Dick Place?		8	'More Than A Woman'
9	Waste Lane?		9	The Big Reunion
10	Hardon Road?		10	Sleeping Beauty

SANDS CENTRE PANTO
All about Cumbria's main annual Christmas pantomime

QUIZ 92

#	Answer
1	Yes, in Barrow-in-Furness
2	No, it's in Oxford
3	Yes, in Cockermouth
4	No, it's in Morecambe
5	Yes, in Carlisle
6	Yes, in Cleator Moor
7	No, it's in Belper
8	No, it's in Doncaster (although there's a Back Lane in Kendal)
9	Yes, in Workington
10	No, it's in Carrickfergus

1	2017's Sleeping Beauty starred Cheryl Ferguson who played Heather Trott in which TV soap?
2	Which local star has appeared in every Sands Centre panto since 2003?
3	Which Britain's Got Talent winner starred with her dog Sully in 2018's The Wizard Of Oz?
4	Actor Peter Dean, who starred in 2003's production of Dick Whittington, is best known for playing which Eastenders character?
5	Which Carlisle-raised star first appeared in the Sands Centre panto in 2013, a year before winning Britain's Got Talent with Collabro?
6	In 2014's Peter Pan Captain Hook was played by Chris Ellison, well known as D.I. Burnside in which long-running police drama?
7	For what reason were the first two days of performances cancelled at the start of 2015's December run?
8	Which actor and dancer, who won Britain's Got Talent and appeared in Waterloo Road and Emmerdale, played Jack in 2016's Jack & The Beanstalk?
9	Which one of the Nolan Sisters appeared in 2013's Snow White & The Seven Dwarfs?
10	Which Three Degrees singer starred as the Fairy Godmother in 2015's production of Cinderella?

1	Which group had a 1986 hit with the song 'Panic' featuring the lyric "panic on the streets of Carlisle"?	**1**	No, it's in Brixham
2	Which Cumbrian town is namechecked in the full-length version of the 1991 top 10 hit 'It's Grim Up North' by The Justified Ancients Of MuMu?	**2**	Yes, in Cleator Moor
3	Whose 1975 number 2 hit 'Moonlighting' mentions "the Carlisle turn off of the M6 motorway"?	**3**	No, it's in Pickering
4	Which singer namechecks Windermere in the lyrics to her 2020 song 'The Lakes' from the album 'Folklore'?	**4**	Yes, one of the Uldale Fells in the Lake District
5	Which former Beatle sings the lyric "Carlisle city never looked so pretty and the Kendal freeway's fast" in the 1973 Wings song 'Helen Wheels'?	**5**	Yes, in Barrow-in-Furness
6	Which famous Noel recorded the song 'There Are Bad Times Just Around The Corner' featuring the lyric "There are home fires smoking from Windermere to Woking"?	**6**	No, it's in Norwich
7	Which former Sex Pistol fronted the group Public Image Ltd. whose song 'Save Me' contains the lyric "Back to mother earth out near Sellafield my nuclear birth"?	**7**	Yes, in Workington
8	Which heavy metal band released the 2019 single 'Solway Firth' from their album 'We Are Not Your Kind'?	**8**	No, it's in Edinburgh
9	Which post-punk band fronted by Mark E. Smith released the 1988 album 'The Frenz Experiment' featuring a song called 'Twister' with the lyric "Up from West Hampstead I visited Keswick"?	**9**	Yes, in Cockermouth
10	Which Cumbrian place gets a mention in an anti-nuclear re-working of Kraftwerk's hit 'Radioactivity' from 1991?	**10**	No, it's in Wolverhampton

PARKS

How much do you know about the parks in the county?

QUIZ 94

1	Eastenders
2	Robbie Dee
3	Ashleigh (Butler)
4	Pete Beale
5	Matt Pagan
6	The Bill
7	Flooding
8	George Sampson
9	Maureen Nolan
10	Sheila Ferguson

1	In which park did the Radio 1 Roadshows take place when they visited Bowness-on-Windermere?
2	Vulcan Park is situated in the centre of which town?
3	Upperby Gala is a park event which takes place by which Carlisle pond?
4	What 'F' is the name of parks in both Keswick and Cockermouth?
5	The Carlisle Fire Show attracts tens of thousands of people to which park each autumn?
6	St James' Park and Trinity Park are both in which town?
7	Which Ulverston park contains a 30-metre zip wire?
8	In which town is Abbots Hall Park?
9	Which Carlisle park played host to the Cumberland Show from 1991-2008?
10	On which park does the Kendal Calling festival now take place?

1	What is the name of Border Television's flagship evening news programme?
2	What was the name of the puppet monkey who would regularly appear with presenter John Myers on *Border Birthdays*?
3	Who was the host of the Border TV-produced game show *Mr & Mrs*?
4	Which presenter and reporter for Border TV for over 30 years died in 2004?
5	From which north east town is the Border region's news output broadcast?
6	Border TV filmed and produced a Sunday version of which Saturday morning kids TV show in 1989 hosted by Shauna Lowry?
7	Where in Carlisle was the children's ITV game show *Crush A Grape* filmed in the 80s?
8	Which music star appeared alongside Rowland Rivron in the Border Television-produced Channel 4 sitcom *The Groovy Fellers*?
9	Which Border TV presenter was one of the original hosts of *GMTV* in 1993?
10	Border TV produced the kids show *K.T.V.* from 1989-1992 featuring which Scottish comedy duo?

#	Answer
1	The Smiths
2	Barrow
3	Leo Sayer
4	Taylor Swift
5	Paul McCartney
6	Noel Coward
7	John Lydon (Johnny Rotten)
8	Slipknot
9	The Fall
10	Sellafield

MUSEUMS

How much do you know about Cumbria's museums?

QUIZ 96

Answers Quiz 94		Museums Quiz 96	
1	The Glebe	1	Which museum near Newby Bridge houses a collection of antique cars?
2	Workington	2	What is the name of the museum of military memorabilia that is housed within Carlisle Castle?
3	Hammond's Pond	3	The building for which Maryport museum was once the Queen's Head pub?
4	Fitz	4	What is the name of the pencil museum in Keswick?
5	Bitts Park	5	Which museum at Carlisle's airport highlights the links between the city and the RAF?
6	Whitehaven	6	What is the full name of the Kendal museum sometimes referred to as MOLLI?
7	Ford Park	7	Which Carlisle museum originally opened in a converted Jacobean mansion in 1893?
8	Kendal	8	The Ruskin Museum, which includes a collection covering the achievements of Donald Campbell, is located in which village?
9	Rickerby Park	9	Which Keswick museum displayed the Reliant Regal van used in *Only Fools And Horses* and the *Chitty Chitty Bang Bang* car as part of its collection, before it closed in 2011?
10	Lowther Deer Park	10	In which town is the Senhouse Roman Museum?

MISSING COLOURS

Can you identify the colour that is
missing in each of these?

#	Question		Answer
1	What colour completes the Houghton restaurant Lounge On The _____ and the Kendal restaurant The _____ House?	1	*Lookaround*
2	Ulverston, Ambleside and Sedbergh all have pubs called The _____ Lion?	2	Eric
3	The Square _____ is a café bar in Keswick?	3	Derek Batey
4	What colour is in the name of Cockermouth estate agent _____ Diamond and Kendal wedding shop _____ Swan?	4	Eric Wallace
5	The boat Donald Campbell attempted to break the world water speed record on Coniston Water with was the _____bird?	5	Gateshead
6	In Ambleside there's a fell with a colour in its name called _____ How?	6	*Ghost Train*
7	This colour features in the name of Ulverston Lingerie shop Boudoir _____ and a house that can be hired by large groups near Mealsgate called The Big _____ House?	7	The Sands Centre
8	Sharing which colour in their names is Carlisle pub Thin _____ Duke and Ambleside hotel The _____ Lion?	8	Jools Holland
9	The _____ Earl in Whitehaven and _____jacket in Carlisle are both drinking establishments?	9	Fiona Armstrong
10	What colour completes the Carlisle gift shop Ashbridge and _____?	10	The Krankies

BUSINESSES
10 questions about Cumbrian industry

QUIZ 98

1	Lakeland Motor Museum
2	Cumbria's Museum of Military Life
3	Maryport Maritime Museum
4	Derwent Pencil Museum
5	Solway Aviation Museum
6	Museum of Lakeland Life and Industry
7	Tullie House Museum and Art Gallery
8	Coniston
9	Cars Of The Stars Museum
10	Maryport

1	Which museum did Carlisle-born Peter Nelson create by bringing together and displaying well-known cars from film and TV in Keswick?
2	Complete the name of the outdoor clothing store in Keswick: George...?
3	What Carlisle business, which first opened as a timber merchants in 1888, has used the slogan 'quality for the home' in more recent times?
4	Which Victorian cook gives her name to the much-celebrated gingerbread sold only at The Grasmere Gingerbread Shop?
5	Which one of Eddie Stobart's sons took over the running of his eponymous company alongside Andrew Tinkler in 2004?
6	Which Cumbria food service was first established in 1878 and has stores in Harrington, Rosehill and Fisher Street?
7	What building company, which was established in Carlisle, was responsible for building The Millennium Stadium in Cardiff?
8	Which Carlisle-based business is the 10th largest building society in the UK?
9	Which independent family-run business runs Tebay motorway services?
10	Which hotel overlooking Ullswater fell into administration in September 2020?

QUIZ 99

PREVIOUS COUNTIES
Before they were part of Cumbria,
what counties were these towns in?

#	Question	#	Answer
1	Appleby?	1	Green
2	Kirkby Lonsdale?	2	Red
3	Barrow-in-Furness?	3	Orange
4	Sedbergh?	4	Purple
5	Egremont?	5	Blue
6	Ulverston?	6	Silver
7	Tebay?	7	Pink
8	Grange-over-Sands?	8	White
9	Keswick?	9	Yellow
10	Millom?	10	Brown

SOME SAY THAT...
These things might be true, but then they might not

#	Answer	#	Question
1	Cars Of The Stars Motor Museum	1	Some say that which of Henry VIII's wives was born at Kendal Castle although evidence suggests the castle would have been in poor condition at the time of her birth?
2	Fisher	2	Some say that an annoyed vicar of which town was sick of his mail being misdirected to Keswick Grange, that he added two hyphenated words to its name to differentiate?
3	Andersons	3	Some say that which Cumbrian road is the best in Britain, specifically scientist Dr Mark Hadley who worked out it has the perfect balance of stretches and corners?
4	Sarah Nelson	4	Some say that aliens are likely to use the lakes in Cumbria as what, with UFO experts claiming in 2009 it could be the reason there are so many UFO sightings in the county?
5	William Stobart	5	Some say that distorting your face as much as possible is the best way to win which annual world championship in Cumbria?
6	Pioneer	6	Some say that which patron saint, whose day is celebrated in many countries around the World, was born in Cumbria in the 5th century?
7	Laing	7	Some say that which King's court was at Carlisle and not Camelot, after this is suggested in a 15th century manuscript poem?
8	The Cumberland Building Society	8	Some say that the last of which canine animal was killed at Humphrey Head near Allithwaite around 1390?
9	Westmorland Motorway Services Ltd.	9	Some say that the oldest what in the world dates back to the 14th century and was discovered in a mine near Caldbeck?
10	Sharrow Bay Country House	10	Some say that a small cloud that rises at the head of which Allerdale valley can predict the weather depending on its behaviour?

1	Westmorland
2	Westmorland
3	Lancashire
4	West Riding of Yorkshire
5	Cumberland
6	Lancashire
7	Westmorland
8	Lancashire
9	Cumberland
10	Cumberland

I hope you're enjoying testing your knowledge of Cumbria. Have you discovered that you actually know loads about the county? Perhaps you've learned one or two gems of information about the area too.

ANSWERS
QUIZ 100

1	Catherine Parr
2	Grange-over-Sands
3	The A591 from Kendal to Keswick
4	Re-fuelling stations
5	World Gurning Championships
6	St. Patrick
7	King Arthur
8	Wolf
9	Railway
10	Borrowdale

I'd love to know what you think about this quiz book. Writing a short review where you purchased it helps independently published writers, such as myself, reach more people who might also enjoy this book, as well as grow as an author through the feedback received. So, if you have a few minutes to contribute your thoughts, or even just a rating, then it would be very much appreciated.. and thank you!

Printed in Great Britain
by Amazon